First Facts®

Our Government

# The City Mayor

by Terri DeGezelle

Consultant:
Michael Reinemer
Director of Communications
National League of Cities
Washington, D.C.

Capstone
press®

Mankato, Minnesota

First Facts is published by Capstone Press,
151 Good Counsel Drive, P.O. Box 669, Mankato, Minnesota 56002.
www.capstonepress.com

*Library of Congress Cataloging-in-Publication Data*
DeGezelle, Terri, 1955–
  The city mayor / by Terri DeGezelle.
    p. cm.—(First facts. Our government)
  Includes bibliographical references and index.
  ISBN-13: 978-0-7368-3685-2 (hardcover)
  ISBN-10: 0-7368-3685-3 (hardcover)
  ISBN-13: 978-0-7368-5153-4 (softcover pbk.)
  ISBN-10: 0-7368-5153-4 (softcover pbk.)
    1. Mayors—United States—Juvenile literature. 2. Municipal government—United States—
Juvenile literature. I. Title. II. Series.
JS356.D44  2005
352.23'214'0973—dc22                                                  2004010937

Summary: An introduction to city government and the role of city mayors.

**Editorial Credits**
Christine Peterson, editor; Jennifer Bergstrom, set designer; Enoch Peterson, book designer;
    Jo Miller, photo researcher

**Photo Credits**
All photographs by Gregg Andersen/Gallery 19 except page 20, Corbis/Roger Ressmeyer

# Table of Contents

## Mayors Lead Cities

Mayors lead most U.S. cities. They are in charge of city governments. Mayors meet with police officers and community leaders. Mayors talk to **citizens** about ideas for their city. Together, they work to make their city better.

5

## City Government

City governments have three parts. Mayors lead cities. **City councils** pass new laws for cities. Courts decide what laws mean.

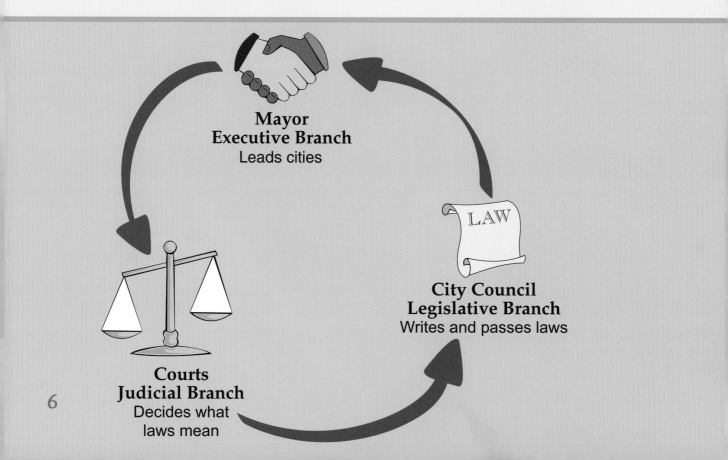

**Mayor
Executive Branch**
Leads cities

LAW

**City Council
Legislative Branch**
Writes and passes laws

**Courts
Judicial Branch**
Decides what
laws mean

Mayors look for ways to improve
their cities. They write and sign laws to
improve city **services**. They listen to
citizens' ideas about **issues**.

## Becoming a Mayor

**Candidates** must follow rules to become mayor. Candidates need to live in the city they want to serve. They must be able to **vote** in that city. In some cities, mayors must be 18 years or older. In other cities, mayors must be at least 21 years old.

**Fact!**
In 1887, Susanna Salter of Argonia, Kansas, became the first U.S. woman mayor.

## People Elect Mayors

People vote for a mayor to lead their city. In some cities, people **elect** mayors to serve two-year **terms**. In large cities, mayors serve for four years. When their terms are over, mayors may be elected again.

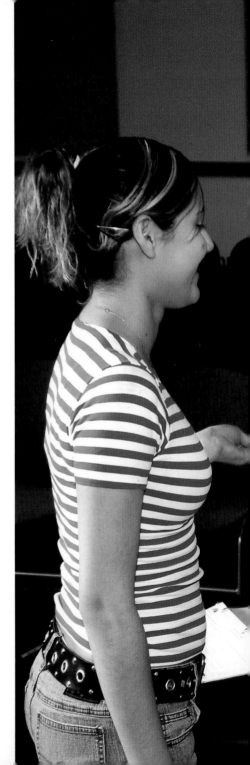

## Mayors Have Many Duties

Mayors work at city halls. At city hall, mayors plan city projects. They find ways to pay for city services, such as police, parks, and water.

Mayors meet with many people. They meet with city workers about street repairs. Mayors find out what work needs to be done.

## City Managers Help Mayors

City managers help mayors with city business. Managers help plan how to spend city money on services, streets, and parks. They work on new laws.

Managers also oversee city services. They plan street projects with mayors and city workers. They make sure cities have clean water.

16

## Mayors Work with Councils

Mayors and city councils help make cities better places to live. Mayors and city councils work together on new laws. They share ideas about city services. They talk about jobs, safety, and other issues.

**Fact!**
The United States has about 19,000 cities, towns, and villages.

17

## Mayors Sign Laws

The mayor and city council pass new laws for their city. At meetings, citizens talk about plans for new laws. The mayor and council then vote. In some cities, mayors vote only when there is a tie. Mayors sign laws to make laws official.

Bosco, a black Labrador retriever, was elected mayor of Sunol, California. This small city had no real government. Some people in the city wanted Bosco to be the mayor. Bosco got more votes than two other people. Bosco was mayor for 11 years.

# Hands On: Write Your Mayor

Many mayors have started book clubs to help kids read. They visit schools and libraries to read books to children. Write a letter to your mayor. Invite your mayor to start a book club in your city or to read books to kids at your school.

## What You Need
paper
pencil or pen
envelope
postage stamp

## What You Do

1. Find your mayor's name and address. You can find your mayor's address on the city's Internet site, in the local newspaper, local library, or in a telephone book.
2. Begin your letter with "Dear Mayor:"
3. Write down your ideas for a mayor's book club for kids. Invite your mayor to visit your school to read a book. You may want to suggest books for the mayor to read.
4. Put your letter in an envelope and write the mayor's address on the front.
5. Place a postage stamp on the upper right-hand corner.
6. Ask an adult to help you mail the letter.

# Glossary

**candidate** (KAN-duh-date)—a person who runs for office

**citizen** (SIT-i-zuhn)—a member of a country, state, or city who has the right to live there

**city council** (SIT-ee KOUN-suhl)—a group of people elected to look after the interests of a city

**elect** (e-LEKT)—to choose someone as a leader by voting

**issue** (ISH-oo)—an idea or need that is talked about by citizens and government leaders

**service** (SUR-viss)—a system or way of providing something useful or necessary; city services include streets, water, and parks.

**term** (TERM)—a set period of time that elected leaders serve in office

**vote** (VOHT)—to make a choice in an election

# Read More

**Flanagan, Alice K.** *Mayors.* Community Workers. Minneapolis: Compass Point Books, 2001.

**Silate, Jennifer.** *Your Mayor: Local Government in Action.* A Primary Source Library of American Citizenship. New York: Rosen Central Primary Source, 2004.

# Internet Sites

FactHound offers a safe, fun way to find Internet sites related to this book. All of the sites on FactHound have been researched by our staff.

**Here's how:**
1. Visit *www.facthound.com*
2. Type in this special code **0736836853** for age-appropriate sites. Or enter a search word related to this book for a more general search.
3. Click on the **Fetch It** button.

FactHound will fetch the best sites for you!

# Index